THESE ARE

THE ANSWERS!

(The Questions are on the back cover...)

1. Nothing!

2. Drunk!

3. Between Joe and Sadie!

4. Joe and Sadie!

5. Open Manhole!

6. December 13, 1938

7. Not buying this thrilling book.

Don't *YOU* make the same mistake!

THE RETURN OF A MAD LOOK AT OLD MOVIES

Screenplay by DICK DE BARTOLO

Cinematography by JACK DAVIS

Directed by NICK MEGLIN

WARNER BOOKS

A Warner Communications Company

For all those dinners that got cold while I worked
without complaint . . .
For all those wonderful suggestions humbly made . . .
For all those long hours of waiting without remorse . . .
This book is proudly dedicated . . .
TO WHOM IT MAY CONCERN!

WARNER BOOKS EDITION

Copyright © 1970 and 1977 by Dick De Bartolo, Jack Davis
and E.C. Publications, Inc.

All rights reserved.
No part of this book may be reproduced without permission. For
information address E.C. Publications, Inc., 485 Madison Ave.,
New York, N.Y. 10022.

ISBN 0-446-86301-7

**Title "MAD" used with permission of its owner,
E.C. Publications, Inc.**

This Warner Books Edition is published by
arrangement with E.C. Publications, Inc.

Warner Books, Inc., 75 Rockefeller Plaza, New York, N.Y. 10019

W A Warner Communications Company

Printed in the United States of America

Not associated with Warner Press, Inc. of Anderson, Indiana

First Printing: July, 1977

10 9 8 7 6 5 4 3 2 1

Contents

FOREWORD

There is always great interest in book authors, and it's both an honor and a privilege to be selected by this author to write a short biography about him for this book. To be chosen for this, in view of my humble background, just goes to show that where else but in a country like ours can an orphan like myself, wretched and poor, pick himself up by his bootstraps and rise above his environment to the point where he can be even *considered* to write a foreword about a man like the author of this book. It wasn't easy, I'll clue you. I mean, how would *you* like to be the only kid out of an orphanage class of 45 that wasn't chosen by foster parents? No, I'm sure you wouldn't like it either. "Too sensitive," I would hear them whisper as they took their Johnnies and Jimmies back to their warm homes and chocolate cake. "Too shy," they would say as that fink Harvey Stonebreaker climbed on a new Schwinn bike his new foster parents bought him. Well, I don't need *anyone* to buy me a bike, Harvey Stonebreaker, wherever you are! I hope you're reading this so you'll know that I made it! I can buy all the bikes I want! With money I earned writing, Harvey! Writing things like forewords for important people like the author of this book, Harvey. People who wouldn't have *anything* to do with the likes of *you!*

But I've gotten off the subject a bit, haven't I? I guess you want to know what happened to me *after* I left the orphanage. Well, I was 18, and I got this job writing scenarios for a stag film producer. My award winning film, "The Plumber's Apprentice," caught the attention of the publisher of Mad Magazine, and, well, here I am.

I've certainly enjoyed this opportunity to write about the author of this book, a real great guy.

Nick Meglin

Associate Editor
Mad Magazine

THE BIGGEST TOP ON EARTH

10

11

12

13

14

16

Oh, I don't know. I just like wearing it, I guess. Ever since I was a boy of 15 I've been wearing make-up. You know how it is . . . .

I know how it is if you're a **girl** of 15, but a boy, I'm afraid, has some problems. It isn't that you're trying to **hide** from someone, is it Rolley?

Hide from someone? What kind of crack is **that!** You certainly know how to hurt a clown!

I'm sorry, Rolley. I've been in too many circus movies where the clown wears make-up to hide from the law and I just figured this was **another** one. How could I have been so wrong? You've got such an **honest face** . . .

Well, this is still not the end! As long as there's **one costume** left . . . as long as there's **one pole** to hold up a piece of canvas . . . as long as there's **one ticket** to sell . . . we're going to have a **show**!

Here's, the report on the damage Bart. There's **not one costume** left, **not one pole** to hold up a piece of canvas, and **all the tickets** have been burned to a crisp.

Bart, the gang is proud of you. A little while ago we were discussing your problems and we said to ourselves "Wouldn't it be a nice gesture to pool all our cash and sell what little we had and turn the money over to you" . . .

Please, Jingo, I'm deeply moved, but that would be **too much.** However . . .

That's what we thought too, so we **didn't do it!**

Thanks **loads!** But what I said still goes— we're going to all pitch in and see this thing through. We're going to have a show **tonight!**

Laydees and gennelmunn . . . welcome to the
Ring-a-ding Bros. Circus. Even though we
are missing a costume or two, we hope you
will enjoy tonight's performances.

To start us off tonight in a dazzling display of horsemanship and marksmanship is our manager, Bart Baker himself! Bart will ride a fast galloping horse around the ring while **shooting light bulbs** out of the mouths of our clown troupe . . .

POW
POW
POW

26

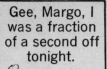

33

34

LIFE·DINGHY

40

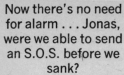

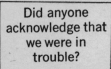

You just want to hear more prayers . . . Well it won't work, Jonas.

Tell me, Mrs. Lilac, why did you decide to take this ill-fated cruise.

It was my children's idea. I'm getting on in years . . . and well, I was getting in the way . . . You know how old folks suddenly seem to be in the way with the younger ones. So they sent me away.

How mean of them! Now, Mrs. Lilac, would you please be a good little old lady, and jump over the side. I'm afraid you're in the way . . .

48

49

The Case Of
THE MAN
WHO
DIED A LOT

54

And if that doesn't work, I'll notify the police! Goodbye!

That's the way her mother was . . . just running over with love and encouragement!

The body is ready, master. All the instruments have been sterilized and laid out for you . . . .

Where?

On the floor, near your feet.

61

63

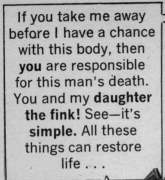

If you take me away before I have a chance with this body, then **you** are responsible for this man's death. You and my **daughter the fink!** See—it's **simple.** All these things can restore life . . .

That's insanity! A pump, some chemicals, tubes . . . and what's this bag of **gum drops** for?

Put that **pancreas** down!

You'd better come along quietly, doctor . . .

MAD SCIENTIST ARRESTED
Doctor Fear Found In Laboratory With Body. Fink Daughter Leads Police to Scene

MAD SCIENTIST GOES TO TRIAL
Daughter Will Act As Witness For D.A. Green Hornet Still at Large

50¢ THE DAILY P

MAD SCIENTIST DIES TONIGHT IN GAS CHAMBER
Fear Has No Fear. Says "I've had gas pains before!"

THE MORNI

65

Doctor Fear was my closest fiend, er, **friend.** He would have wanted me to have something to **remember him by,** like his body.

My good man, do you think you can just march in off the street and claim a body **just like that?** Though it is extinguished, it is not something one gives away. It is still a wonderful mechanism . . .

Here's five dollars . . .

Take **all you want!**

I must follow the doctor's notes exactly . . . "Heat instruments to 98.6 degrees, connect 3 flashlight batteries to one medium sized body, fold in three cans of condensed blood . . ."

You would think out of four clocks you would find **one** that works . . .

68

Oh, the foot bone connected to the leg bone . . .
The leg bone connected to the knee bone . . .
The knee bone connected to the garden hose . . .

There . . . all the necessary parts have been **replaced.** Now to put his brain under my command with a **bolt of lightning . . .**

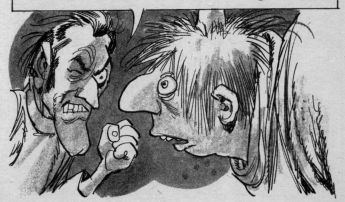

75

76

Well, there's something mighty strange going on. **All** the 40 people killed in this insane murder spree played some part in the execution of your father. I think it's part of some fiendish plot. I think your father's experiments in bringing back life might have **succeeded.** I think your father is **still alive** and is responsible for those murders.
Quit beating around the bush and tell me what you **think!**
PRESS

I think we should go back to the laboratory and search for a **secret room** your father may be hiding in.
And if he's not there we can always **neck . . .**

79

Periscopes
Out of the
Blue

91

I don't care if he has a cute appendicitis or **adorable adenoids,** I need him at his station. Every man has a job on this ship and no one can be **replaced, least of all** Fishman! He's the only **laundry room man** in the Navy who knows how to keep **shorty pajamas** soft and comfy!

But Captain, unless his appendix is removed immediately, Fishman will **die.** And we don't have a **doctor** on board.

If he dies, you don't **need** a doctor, silly! And as Pharmacist's Mate, **you** must know what to do . . .

I don't have the **instruments,** the **operating table,** the **sterilization equipment,** and with Fishman not at his job, I don't even have **clean sheets!**

We'll leave the choice to **him** . . .

Listen, Hank, I know you're in pain, but you **gotta** hear me. It's **your** choice to make! Either Gordon here **operates,** or we put you in a torpedo tube and **shoot you over** to a ship with a doctor. What'll it be, boy?

I'll take my chances with **Gordon,** Sir. I've **heard** about your aim with the torpedoes!

99

105

108

THE INVENTING FOOL

110

111

115

And so, Tom Edison began his work. But this time as a man, and not as a boy. And his mother encouraged him as a man, and not as a boy, which didn't help his Oedipus complex too much! She rented him back his room where he worked 24 hours a day, sometimes even longer . . .

Tom, this is ridiculous. You've been working too long, too hard. You don't even stop to **eat**. Let me **sell** you a bowl of soup . . .

I can't stop now. I have to **perfect** this latest experiment!

What's to **perfect**? That thing has been burning brightly for days now. It's a perfect **electric light bulb!**

It's supposed to be a **telephone!**

But Tom continued his work and soon began to amaze his associates with one invention after another . . .

121

122

Tom began lecturing on his theory of generating electricity . . .

Gentlemen, strange as it sounds, I actually **generate electricity** when I pet this cat!

Mr. Edison, will the electricity generated be powerful enough to do anything?

No. And this is where all of you can help me. We need a greater source of power to produce enough electrical force to harness and utilize. Do any of you know where I can get a **15 foot pussy cat?**

Preposterous!

Tom, more determined than ever, began his endless work once again . . .

125

That too. My little boy has put down his teddy bear and picked up the world. All your years of hard work and sacrifice have not been in vain. Despite the cruelty of others, the jeering of your friends and neighbors, the high cost of rent and soup, you carried on your endless search for inventions that would make life more pleasant for others.

127

FLIGHT 1313

132

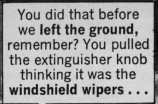

135

You co-pilots are **power hungry,** do you know that, McGee? It's time to sit and wait and hope and think back about the events that brought us to this crucial, suspenseful moment! Can't you see the FLASHBACK indicator lighting up? **Every** Hollywood-built plane has one!

Oh, I see. My thoughts are drifting back . . . back to Dorothy. Before we took off I was thinking of walking out on her and the 10 kids. But if we make it out of this alive, I'm going back to her. I might even **marry** her. Bachelor life has been no fun with 10 kids. . . .

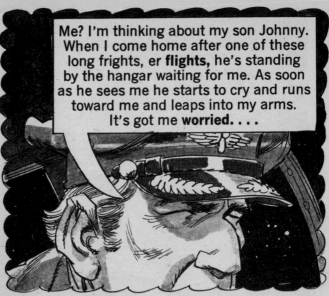

Me? I'm thinking about my son Johnny. When I come home after one of these long frights, er **flights,** he's standing by the hangar waiting for me. As soon as he sees me he starts to cry and runs toward me and leaps into my arms. It's got me **worried. . . .**

Worried? What on earth for? That sounds **wonderful!**

Johnny's **27 years old!**

I see what you mean. But I think we've spent **enough time** on our own flashbacks, Captain. Shouldn't we go back to the cabin and pick up the thoughts of some of the **passengers?**

By God, McGee, you're catching on **fast!** We'll make a Hollywood pilot out of you yet!

I was going to **divorce** Harry. I didn't want to be **tied down** anymore. That's a laugh! Here I am, Audrey Tawdry on a flight to freedom, and the person I miss **most** is Harry. If I get out of this alive, I'm **going back** to Harry. And I'm never going to mention freedom to him again! I'll just **sneak out** nights without his knowing it. . . .

What a joke! I desert from the Army because I'm a **coward.** I'm afraid to face the possibility of dying. So what do I do? I get on a plane facing death! If I get out of this alive I'm **going back** to my Company and sign up for a **dangerous mission**—like Recruiting at the Berkeley campus . . .

Attention, ladies and gentlemen. This is the Captain. While you were all having your **revealing thoughts,** the two fires went out and we were able to locate a small airfield in the area. The landing is going to be **rough** and **dangerous.** When the plane is in **perfect condition** my landings are rough and dangerous, so you can imagine what **this** one's going to be like! Hang on, cause **here we go. . . .**

147

148

149

BLAZING
BLADES

152

153

154

155

That's **swashbuckler.** I'll get right to the point. If you'll do a little job for me, I'll provide you with another ship. The daughter of the Duke of Fricasse, Lady Lasagna, is leaving the Chateau Croissant for Turkey aboard the Golden Goose . . .

Do you mind if **I order some food?** I'm suddenly very **hungry** . . .

Lady Lasagna is wearing a certain **gold locket** that I want. This is an **exact replica** of it. You are to intercept her ship and switch lockets without her knowing. When you return with it, I will hand you the ownership papers of the ship you will be sailing.

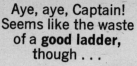

163

164

167

171

173

174

175

CAMPUS CAPERS

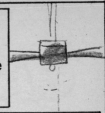

181

Hi, folks. We want to thank you all for coming. You may not see too much shine and shimmer in tonight's makeshift show, but what you will see is a lot of heart. These kids knew what they had to do and they delivered, so don't be too hard on us. Now let's go with our opening number. Take it away sweet Sue Meyer and dashing Don Holden singing "I Can Row, Canoe?" Raise the makeshift curtain, Hal . . .

Frank and Barbara, get ready for your **locomotive** number. Dave, you got the **cattle** ready for the "Rodeo Stampede" sketch? Joan, when you do the dream sequence in the "Fly To Love" number with Stan, don't stand too close to the **propeller** We've already lost Jonas! Bill, you blowing up the **zeppelin?** Good! Arnie, check out the **harem girls** for the "Ali Baba" number!

189